Since 1888, *National Geographic* magazine has provided its readers a wealth of information and helped us understand the world in which we live. Insightful articles, supported by gorgeous photography and impeccable research, bring the mission of the National Geographic Society front and center: to inspire people to care about the planet. The *Explore* series delivers *National Geographic* to you in the same spirit. Each of the books in this series presents the best articles on popular and relevant topics in an accessible format. In addition, each book highlights the work of National Geographic Explorers, photographers, and writers. Explore the world of *National Geographic*. You will be inspired.

ON THE COVER
Ceremonial animal-spirit incense burner used by the Maya

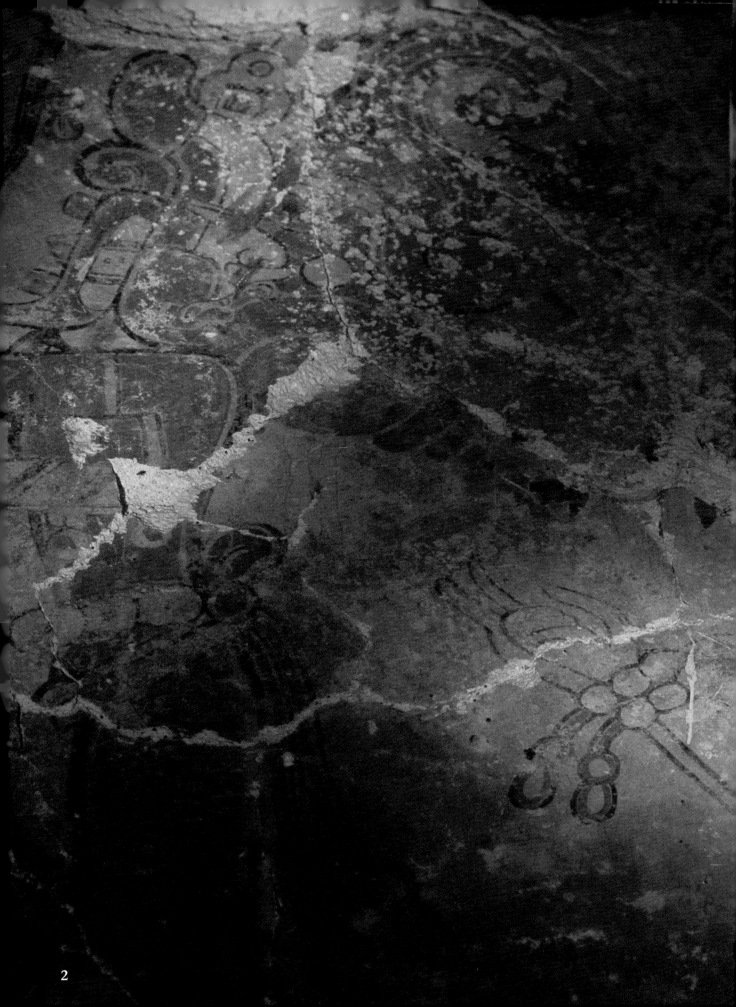

2

THE MAYA

4 **Letter from the Editors**

5 **Rediscovering the Maya** *By Heather Pringle*
A brooding fog. A remote jungle. Ruins from an ancient civilization. Join explorers and scientists as they unearth the secrets of the mysterious Maya.

14 **The Birth of Kings** *By Heather Pringle*
The early Maya lords were godlike figures to their subjects. After all, they built a great civilization without modern tools or knowledge from the outside world.

18 **Explorer's Journal with William Saturno** *By William Saturno*
Meet National Geographic Explorer and respected archaeologist William Saturno. Read a firsthand account of his discoveries in the remote Guatemalan jungle.

24 **Lords of War** *By Heather Pringle*
Great Maya cities rose to heights of glory and then collapsed, destroyed by war and forces beyond the control of their powerful leaders.

28 **A Gift from the Gods: Chocolate**
By A.R. Williams
Imagine using cacao—chocolate—as money. The Maya did, and they also gave the world one of its favorite drinks.

30 **Trade and Intrigue in the North**
By Heather Pringle
The trading powerhouses in what is now southern Mexico were the last of the great Maya cities. It took hundreds of years for the end to come.

36 **Monuments of the Maya**
Models of three pyramids from three different locations and periods can tell us about the history and culture of the Maya.

38 **Document-Based Question**
How did the Spanish help bring an end to the Maya civilization?

LETTER FROM THE EDITORS

Between 1000 B.C. and A.D. 1500, one powerful Maya city-state after another rose to power in parts of present-day Mexico and Central America. Palenque and Cival, Tikal and Calakmul, San Bartolo and El Mirador, Chichén Itzá and Mayapán: all had their time of great glory. But by the 1500s, the last of the great Maya powers had collapsed, and the Spanish were beginning their long, bloody conquest of the region.

Maya society was one of the most advanced in the ancient and early modern world. The Maya were skilled farmers whose bountiful harvests fed great cities. They were daring merchants who carried goods such as gold, cacao, jade, feathers, and salt along the rivers and coastlines. They were gifted stoneworkers who raised giant pyramids using only the most basic tools. They were artists who painted colorful murals to honor their gods and kings. They were brilliant scholars, scientists, and astronomers who mapped the stars and planets, invented a complex writing system, and created a calendar almost as accurate as calendars today.

For hundreds of years, no one knew much about the Maya. They kept written records, but archaeologists could not read their script. The ruins of Maya cities were buried in remote jungles, and many sites were long lost. But early 20th-century discoveries began to unlock many secrets of this fascinating civilization. To this day researchers continue to unearth new evidence that has changed their thinking about the rise and fall of the great cities.

Many recent discoveries are described in the articles you are about to read. Through the words and photographs of National Geographic writers and photographers, you will learn about how the Maya kings gained immense power. As you read, catch the spirit of adventure and discovery. As you learn, appreciate the rich heritage of the Maya people, who still live, work, and worship in the land of their ancestors.

MAYA BALL PLAYER
This clay figurine displays the thick padding Maya ball players wore to protect themselves from a heavy ball and fierce competitors.

4

Rediscovering the Maya

BY HEATHER PRINGLE

Adapted from "Rediscovering the Maya: Lost and Found,"
by Heather Pringle, in National Geographic's *Mysteries of the Maya*, 2008

ANCIENT KING
This elaborate jade mask
was found in the tomb of
Pakal, ruler of the Maya
city-state of Palenque.

FOR CENTURIES, the ruins of the great Maya cities lay beneath a thick layer of forest growth. Modern researchers have only just begun to understand this complex civilization. Still, much about the Maya remains yet to be discovered.

KING OF A LOST WORLD

In the year A.D. 615, the boy king Pakal took the throne of Palenque (pah-LEHN-kay). The people of this Maya city-state believed that their king had the power to summon rain for their parched fields and bring order to a troubled world. But no one could say how long the boy would survive. In nearby kingdoms, enemy lords schemed and plotted, seeking signs of weakness in the 12-year-old ruler. Just four years earlier, a powerful king named Scroll Serpent had ordered his army to attack Palenque. Crossing several rivers in the dry season, his warriors had sacked the city. These were dangerous times.

Pakal, however, knew how to listen and take advice. His mother came from Palenque's old royal family and had ruled until her son came of age. Following her guidance, he made alliances with distant lords. He outsmarted his enemies on the battlefield and restored Palenque's power and importance. In years of peace he commanded his subjects to beautify the city. Palenque became one of the most elegant capitals of the Maya world. When Pakal finally died after 68 years on the throne, his subjects mourned him deeply. They bathed his body in sacred **cinnabar** and adorned it with precious jade.

History now knows Pakal as one of the greatest of all Maya kings and the Maya as one of the world's greatest civilizations. But for centuries, the Maya world was a lost world. Its ruins were buried. Its story was shrouded in mystery.

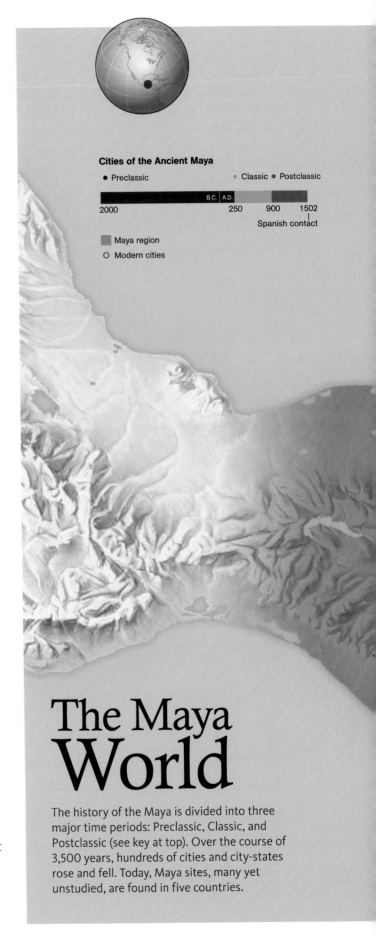

Cities of the Ancient Maya

● Preclassic   ● Classic ● Postclassic

| | | | B.C. | A.D. | | | |
2000   250   900   1502

Spanish contact

■ Maya region
○ Modern cities

The Maya World

The history of the Maya is divided into three major time periods: Preclassic, Classic, and Postclassic (see key at top). Over the course of 3,500 years, hundreds of cities and city-states rose and fell. Today, Maya sites, many yet unstudied, are found in five countries.

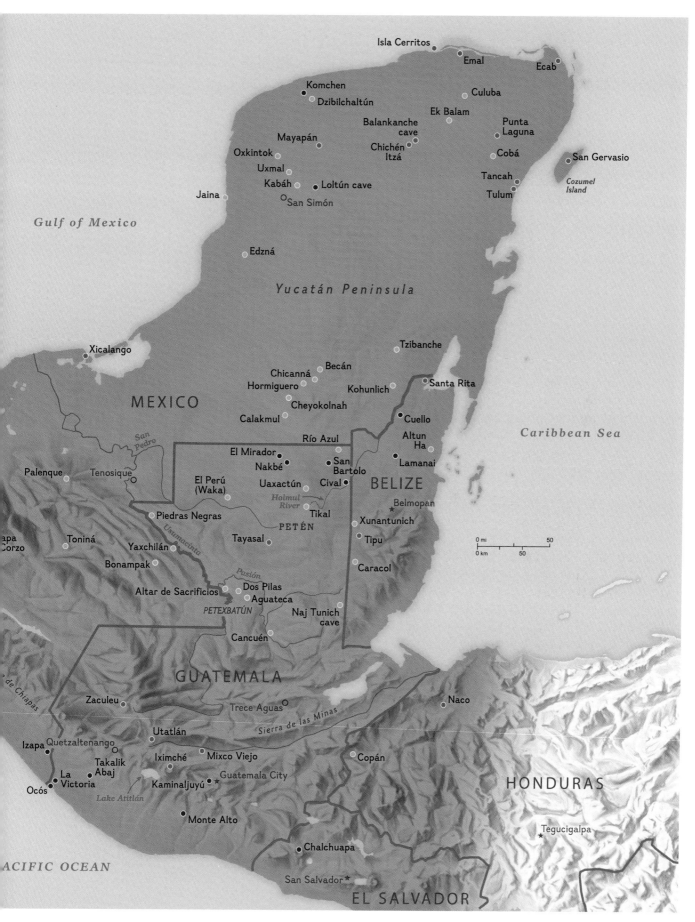

Isla Cerritos

Emal

Ecab

Komchen

Culuba

Dzibilchaltún

Ek Balam

Balankanche
cave

Punta
Laguna

Mayapán

Oxkintok

Chichén
Itzá

Cobá

San Gervasio

Uxmal

Tancah

*Cozumel
Island*

Kabáh

Loltún cave

Tulum

Jaina

San Simón

Gulf of Mexico

Edzná

Yucatán Peninsula

Xicalango

Tzibanche

Becán

Chicanná

Santa Rita

Hormiguero

Kohunlich

MEXICO

Cheyokolnah

Cuello

Calakmul

Altun
Ha

Caribbean Sea

Río Azul

El Mirador

San
Bartolo

Lamanai

Nakbé

*San
Pedro*

Palenque

Tenosique

El Perú
(Waka)

Uaxactún

Cival

BELIZE

*Holmul
River*

Belmopan

Piedras Negras

Tikal

Xunantunich

Toniná

PETÉN

Usumacinta

Yaxchilán

Tipu

Bonampak

Pasión

Caracol

Altar de Sacrificios

Dos Pilas

Aguateca

PETEXBATÚN

Naj Tunich
cave

Cancuén

0 mi   50

0 km   50

*apa
Corzo*

GUATEMALA

de Chiapas

Zaculeu

Trece Aguas

Naco

Utatlán

Sierra de las Minas

Izapa

Quetzaltenango

Iximché

Mixco Viejo

Copán

Takalik
Abaj

HONDURAS

La
Victoria

Guatemala City

Ocós

Kaminaljuyú

Lake Atitlán

Monte Alto

Tegucigalpa

Chalchuapa

ACIFIC OCEAN

San Salvador

EL SALVADOR

FORMER GLORY
Found in the 1930s, this giant mask made of
fine plaster once topped a Maya pyramid.
During the centuries it lay undiscovered,
it was largely reclaimed by the forest near
Piedras Negras in Petén, Guatemala.

THE MYSTERIOUS MAYA

Only recently have archaeologists and others begun piecing together the dramatic history of the Maya world. It is a history rich in plots, conquest, and splendor. **Excavations** at vine-covered cities and studies of the writing on crumbling stones are shedding light on the Maya: their kings and queens, artists and astronomers, merchants, farmers, and craftspeople. Researchers continue to marvel at the richness of the culture they are uncovering.

"It is a world of magnificent artistic and intellectual achievement," says David Freidel, an American archaeologist. Armed with new technology, researchers are unearthing clues to long-puzzling questions about the Maya. Who exactly were they? How did they forge such a sophisticated civilization in the heart of a tangled jungle? What brought their great cities to the heights of greatness? What plunged the Maya into decline and collapse?

The world knew almost nothing about the Maya 200 years ago. Tropical forest had overgrown many of their ancient cities. European invaders had burned all but a few of their books, written on the bark of fig trees. But in the late 1700s, a report of strange ruins at Palenque reached the Spanish king. Intrigued, he sent a military captain, Antonio del Rio, to investigate and report back.

When del Rio arrived at Palenque on May 5, 1787, a dense fog cloaked the ancient site. The officer returned 13 days later with 79 workers and began hacking away at the vegetation. He pushed tumbled stone from doorways and roamed dark underground passages. He collected broken statues and earthenware jars. He marveled at the city's **aqueduct** system and the vast sprawl of ruined buildings.

Del Rio struggled to explain how such a magnificent place had risen in the remote jungle. He finally decided that a band of ancient Romans or Greeks or Phoenicians once conquered the region. They stayed just long enough to teach local inhabitants the basics of architecture and art. Given what del Rio knew, this seemed like a logical explanation.

A TEMPLE FOR ETERNITY
The ruined temple of Palenque,
in southern Mexico, bears silent
witness to the greatness of the city
and the people it served. Parts of
the temple date back to 226 B.C.

A STORY IN STONE
These Maya glyphs, a form of pictorial writing, were found in Copán, in present-day Honduras. They tell of events in Maya history.

DISCOVERING THE TRUE MAYA

Nearly a century passed before scientists undertook serious study of the **enigmatic** ruins at Palenque and hundreds of other sites. In 1881 Alfred Maudslay, a British explorer, began investigating the markings on the ancient stones found at most of the sites. He realized that scholars needed detailed photographs, drawings, and plaster molds to begin figuring out these mysterious **glyphs**. Maudslay traveled throughout Central America. He once borrowed a jail cell to set up a photographic lab. His careful recording of the markings was the beginning of modern archaeological research on the Maya. This research revealed no trace of foreign invaders from Rome or Greece. Researchers came to agree that the roots of the ancient Maya civilization lay deep in the Americas.

By the 1920s, archaeologists were longing for new clues to the origins and fate of the Maya. They realized that they needed help from scientists in many different fields. Expeditions to Mexico and Central America began to include botanists, zoologists, geologists, and folklorists. Often traveling by mule along remote jungle trails, these expeditions looked for previously unknown Maya capitals and carried out detailed excavations of many sites. Their research fired the public imagination. Popular writers began portraying the Maya as peaceful farmers, ruled by learned astronomer-priests.

The vision of the Maya as a peaceful society quickly faded when researchers began unlocking the secrets of Maya glyphs. In 1960, an American art historian figured out that dates carved on large stone monuments at one site recorded important events in the lives of individual kings and queens. Such advances led to the understanding of hundreds of glyphs. Piece by piece, researchers reconstructed the rich history of a civilization as warlike and political as any. It was a history filled with triumphs and trials, with royal ambition, betrayal, and hatred.

We now know that the Maya created one of the most advanced societies in the ancient world. Its engineers erected towering stone-clad pyramids without using iron tools or wheels. Its scholars grasped the notion of zero and used a place system for numbers. Its astronomers charted the moon, stars, and planets and calculated cycles of time with remarkable accuracy. (The Maya calculation of the lunar month is just 24 seconds off from the time recorded by today's clocks.) And each year we learn more about the sophistication of Maya civilization as scientists make use of new technologies. These include electron microscopes and satellites that record images of the impressive raised highways built by the Maya.

Still, many questions remain. Where and when did the Maya build their earliest cities? How did they feed their huge populations? How did the first Maya kings gain such great power? Answers to these questions too may come in the years ahead.

THINK ABOUT IT! ||||||||||||||||||||||||||||||

1 **Form and Support Opinions** Of all the discoveries made over hundreds of years, what one discovery do you think was the most important to learning about the Maya? Give reasons for your choice.

2 **Analyze Cause and Effect** Why do you think it took scientists hundreds of years to begin understanding Maya civilization?

BACKGROUND & VOCABULARY

aqueduct *n.* (AK-wuh-duhkt) a human-built channel for carrying flowing water

cinnabar *n.* (SIHN-uh-bahr) a red mineral

enigmatic *adj.* (eh-nihg-MA-tik) difficult to understand; mysterious

excavation *n.* (ex-kuh-VAY-shuhn) the act or process of digging to uncover buried items

glyph *n.* (glihf) a pictorial character used in a system of writing

The Birth of Kings

BY HEATHER PRINGLE

Adapted from "Saga in Stone: The Birth of Kings,"
by Heather Pringle, in National Geographic's *Mysteries of the Maya*, 2008

GOD OF CORN
This statue of the maize
god was reconstructed
from a jumble of fallen
stone at the city of Copán.

IN THE ANCIENT MAYA CITY OF SAN BARTOLO
2,100 years ago, an artist set down his brush. The lord of San
Bartolo had brought him to this private pyramid room and
commanded him to paint the sacred story of creation. The
artist had obeyed, working on murals that few eyes would ever
see. On one wall, the young god of corn came up from the
underworld. Standing back, the artist studied his masterpiece.

BIRTH OF A CITY

The ancestors of this Maya artist had arrived in
the lowlands of Guatemala thousands of years
ago. They were following the course of winding
rivers. In the deep tropical forests they found
a lush, green world. Marshes and swamps cut
through the forest. It was in many ways a land of
extremes. From May to November each year, rain
sheeted down. Water filled streams and pooled
in swampy lowlands and lakes. In February,
however, the rains stopped. Over the next
few months, water grew precious. The artist's
ancestors wisely settled near the most reliable
sources of water. There they hunted game, tended
small gardens, and gathered food from the
marshes in the area.

The new forest dwellers carried with them the
plants they had experimented with for thousands
of years. Of these, they most loved **maize**,
or corn. The ears were sweet and starchy, and
the long stalks must have seemed particularly
beautiful to Maya eyes. Moreover, the life cycle
of the plant recalled that of human beings. The
green sprouts reminded the Maya of the birth of
humans from the ground, as told in their sacred
stories. And the cutting of the stalks at harvest
reminded them that all living things must die in
the great cycle of life.

Corn was a delicate crop that quickly withered
in times of drought. The tender shoots needed
steady, moderate rainfall. This posed a serious
problem for early farmers in the lowlands.
There rainfall stopped for months. To grow
golden fields of corn, the Maya had to time their
planting with the end of the dry season.

The earliest Maya lords were likely the best
farmers, who closely observed the world around
them and won respect for their skills. "One of the
keys to who became the privileged," says Robert
Sharer, an American archaeologist, "had to do
with practical knowledge . . . when to plant corn,
how to plant it, where to plant it, and how to
nurture it."

By training their eyes on the eastern sky, the
lords began to note the exact position of the
sunrise on the spring and fall **equinoxes**. With
these observations, Maya lords started marking
the rhythms of nature. The life-giving rains,
they discovered, often returned to the central
lowlands close to the same date each year. That
date was May 10, the day the sun passed directly
overhead in the sky.

Such knowledge was power. In time, some
lords began to demand grand new public
stages to perform ceremonies. In the ancient
city of Cival (see-VAHL), farmers had gathered
for generations on the city's sprawling plaza.
They watched the lords perform sacred rites to
summon rains for the corn shoots in the fields.
With each successful harvest, the reputation
of Cival's lords grew. Many in the city came to
believe that their lords had supernatural powers.

During the eighth century B.C., Cival's lords
ordered the farmers to **quarry** stone for a large
pyramid. The men agreed, fearing that refusal
would bring drought, scorched crops, and long
months of hunger. Swinging heavy picks and
stone hammers, they split slabs of limestone.
They hauled the stone to a massive construction
site on the plaza. Slowly the farmers raised a
pyramid that was as tall as a four-story building.

15

ANCIENT MASK
Another Maya city from the Preclassic period was Lamanai, located in present-day Belize. The Temple of the Mask there features a 13-foot high stone mask.

Directly opposite, at a spot chosen by the lord along the eastern edge of the plaza, they built a long platform topped by three buildings.

The ruler of Cival had designed these structures as an **astronomical observatory**. On the spring and fall equinoxes, the sun rose from a point precisely at the center of the eastern platform. On May 10, the day the rains usually began, the sun rose behind one of the three buildings. It did so again on August 3, when the second wave of rains returned. Using this grand architectural calendar, the lords of Cival could predict when best to make offerings to the gods and plant the fields.

As the fame of Cival's lords spread, other buildings rose in the center of the expanding city. The most impressive was a 108-foot-tall pyramid that sprawled over an acre. Perched along one edge of the plaza, this huge structure dominated the entire city. To decorate its steep walls, artisans crafted huge masks portraying the fearsome faces of the sky and rain gods. The pyramid was surely an impressive sight.

In all likelihood, the imposing structure served as a stage for sacred reenactments of the birth of the maize god. To those standing in front of it, the pyramid faces both the rising sun and the direction of rain-bearing storms. Moreover, like the top of a high hill, it naturally attracts lightning. Framed by bolts of fire, a king dressed in brilliantly colored clothes may well have stood or danced atop this great stage at the start of the rainy season. He would have looked to the people like a god reaching into the heavens to bring rains to a dry land.

THE RISE OF OTHER GREAT CITIES

Many other cities were being built along the marshlands and rivers. Their rulers too erected pyramids and claimed supernatural powers. "The maize god became the symbol for the Maya kings," says Robert Sharer. At San Bartolo, the master artist chose this relationship between king and god as the theme of his great mural. Along the walls of the pyramid chamber, he showed both the creation of the world by the maize god and the coronation of the king. To the faithful, god and king were one.

No early Maya kings wielded more power than those who ruled the ancient city of El Mirador. Surrounded by dense forest even today, El Mirador lies in a broad, swampy basin in northern Guatemala. The region has little fresh, flowing water. But during the rainy season water pools in temporary swamps bordered by ridges. Maya farmers cleverly adapted to this watery land. They farmed the ridges and dug muck from marshes and lakes to fertilize their fields and bring forth a good harvest.

Wealthy from these bountiful harvests, El Mirador's kings took control of neighboring cities and founded what some call the first Maya state. They commanded their subjects to build a network of crushed-rock **causeways** stretching north, south, and east through the jungle. By the first century A.D., El Mirador ruled an area about the size of the state of Rhode Island.

At the heart of this early state, El Mirador became one of the largest cities the Maya ever built. Like Cival, El Mirador had giant pyramids and astronomical observatories. The city's greatest architectural wonder was the Danta complex, which towered 230 feet above the plaza. It was the largest stone building ever constructed by the Maya.

El Mirador paid a steep price for its glories. The city's builders spread thick layers of plaster over the walls and floors of private houses and public buildings. This elegant touch sparked an early ecological crisis. To make plaster, the Maya heated blocks of stone at high temperatures in charcoal-fired ovens. "It takes a massive amount of green wood to make charcoal," notes archaeologist Justine Shaw. El Mirador's wood-hungry builders slashed vast tracts of forest. During the wet season, rains washed soil from the bare lands into marshes and lagoons. Eventually the marshes and lagoons were filled in. Farmers were no longer able to dig the muck for fertilizer. Their fields ceased to produce crops. As food supplies decreased, so did the population.

By the middle of the third century A.D., the once sprawling city of El Mirador was a ghost town. But elsewhere in the forested lowlands, powerful new dynasties in other cities were beginning to transform Maya society.

THINK ABOUT IT! ||||||||||||||||||||||||||||||||

1 **Summarize** Explain in your own words how some Maya farmers became lords and leaders of their people.

2 **Analyze Cause and Effect** How did achievements in astronomy contribute to the greatness of Maya culture?

2 **Find Main Ideas and Details** San Bartolo, Cival, and El Mirador were all great Maya cities. Identify something unique about each, citing details from the article.

BACKGROUND & VOCABULARY

astronomical *adj.* (as-truh-NAHM-ih-kuhl) related to astronomy, the study of the physical properties of objects in outer space

causeway *n.* (KAWZ-way) a long, raised highway

equinox *n.* (EE-kwuh-nahks) the two times of year (about March 21 and September 23) when the sun crosses the equator and day and night are of approximately equal length

maize *n.* (MAYZ) another name for corn

observatory *n.* (uhb-ZUR-vuh-tor-ee) a place equipped for studying objects in outer space such as planets and stars

quarry *v.* (KWOR-ee) to cut into rock or ground to obtain materials such as stone

EXPLORER'S JOURNAL

with William Saturno

Adapted from "The Dawn of Maya Gods and Kings," by
William Saturno, in *National Geographic*, January 2006

MESSY WORK
Archaeologist William Saturno
creates a small shower of stone
fragments as he scrapes loose
material near a Maya painting
in Xultun, Guatemala. Saturno
discovered even more impressive
murals at nearby San Bartolo.

National Geographic Explorer and archaeologist William Saturno's discoveries have rewritten the history of the Maya. In this Explorer's Journal, Saturno discusses his work in his own words.

MASTERPIECE UNCOVERED

The two artists worked by torchlight and morning sunshine. Perhaps they were twins, like the twin artist-scribes of Maya myth. Certainly they had trained for their task since youth, copying the books that held the sacred stories. Now, under their brushes, the gods and their acts of creation burst to life on polished plaster.

The finished paintings covered at least two walls of a room at the base of a pyramid. The masterpiece had two purposes. One was to honor the gods. The other was to illustrate that the king **derived** his power from those gods. After only a few decades the room was buried beneath a larger pyramid, which honored a new ruler in the ancient city we know as San Bartolo. There the paintings remained, hidden in the Guatemalan jungle, for more than 2,000 years. I was the fortunate one to uncover the **murals**.

HIDDEN PYRAMID
Saturno discovered the San Bartolo murals painted on walls in the pyramid illustrated above. The different levels of the pyramid were built centuries apart and eventually covered by the thick rain forest.

NEW REVELATIONS

The project began in March 2001 with a stroke of pure luck. I ducked into a trench that looters had cut into the pyramid and saw the face of the maize god looking over his shoulder at a beautiful maiden. I longed to see the rest of the mural. But it took two years of planning to ensure that further excavation wouldn't damage it. In March 2003 I began to dig a narrow tunnel inside the mural room, paralleling a long wall. I left undisturbed the **mortar** and stone covering the paintings. When the tunnel was finished, I began to chip away the remaining stones that concealed the mural.

It was as if an ancient Maya book had been spread open before me, recounting the birth of the Maya world. Parts of the story were familiar from two texts that had been written during a later period. But these paintings, more than a thousand years older, told the same tale with startling sophistication. Clearly Maya painting had achieved glory several centuries before the great Maya works of the seventh century, which had already been unearthed.

The far end of the mural held another surprise. Some scholars thought that at this early stage in Maya history **city-states** were not yet full-fledged kingdoms. But here was a king, named and titled, receiving his crown. This mural **upended** much of what we thought we knew about the early Maya.

KINGS' GOD
This part of the San Bartolo mural depicts the son of the maize god. Not only was he the son of a god—he was also the patron deity, or main god, of Maya kings.

21

A KING IS FOUND

Almost a mile west of the painted room lay an actual king, the earliest known Maya royal burial. In 2005, Guatemalan archaeologist Mónica Pellecer Alecio dug beneath a small pyramid and found signs of the sealed tomb. Fearing looters working nearby, her crew excavated 24 hours a day, sleeping in shifts.

Just after 2 a.m. on the third day, 20 workmen using a giant wooden lever cut from a tree in the forest moved the heavy stones that sealed the tomb. Beneath lay the bones of a man. The offerings buried with him included a delicate frog-shaped bowl and a vase bearing a figure of Chac, the rain god. On the man's chest rested a curved jade plaque—a symbol of Maya royalty.

Just as the team removed the figure of Chac, the clouds opened and the region's worst dry season in a decade came to an end.

THINK ABOUT IT! |||||||||||||||||||||||||||||||

1 **Make Generalizations** Based on the information in this article, what personal qualities are important in an archaeologist?

2 **Pose and Answer Questions** On page 23, you can read a National Geographic interview with William Saturno. What two questions would you have asked him?

3 **Draw Conclusions** How were religion and government connected for the Maya?

BACKGROUND & VOCABULARY

city-state *n.* an independent country made up of a city and the area that surrounds it

derive *v.* to obtain something from a specific source

mortar *n.* (MOR-tur) a material such as cement that hardens and is used to construct stone or brick buildings

mural *v.* (MYUR-uhl) a painting that is applied directly to a wall

upend *v.* (uhp-EHND) to turn over; change completely

DIFFICULT TERRAIN
William Saturno and colleagues install equipment on the side of a pyramid. This equipment helps monitor the temperature and humidity inside a mural chamber.

National Geographic Interviews William Saturno

National Geographic: What did you want to be when you were growing up?

William Saturno: I always wanted to be an archaeologist. As a child I loved dirt. In fact, as my mother tells it, there was often no separating me from it. I used to conduct "excavations" in my backyard using my mother's silverware. I never did find anything of note, other than spoons left bent and twisted from my previous excavations.

NG: What inspired you to dedicate your life to archaeology?

William Saturno: The people. I love the work I do, the puzzles, the mystery. But more important I love the people I get to work with. I have spent the last 12 years working in northeastern Guatemala, and the passion of my colleagues, students, excavators, and their families is inspiring. I see being an archaeologist as both a great privilege and a great responsibility. I have been entrusted with the recovery, interpretation, and preservation of the material remains of the past, with the history of an ancient people, and the heritage of its modern descendants.

NG: What has been your favorite experience in the field?

William Saturno: My favorite and most challenging experience in the field was excávating the San Bartolo murals. Being the first person to see them after more than 2,000 years, uncovering them bit by bit, with each part more beautiful than the last, is an experience unlikely to be matched.

Following the excavation of the west wall mural, a number of important visitors helicoptered in to see the murals firsthand. One important visitor arrived by land, having hitched a ride with our weekly supply truck. After four hours bouncing through the dense forest, Ian Graham, the great Maya explorer and one of the men I most admire, emerged from the mud-covered pick-up.

As we entered the cramped tunnel, Ian's eyes welled up with tears at the sight of the painting before him. He sat silently, taking in the masterpiece. Eventually he uttered, "This is the greatest, really, the greatest find."

LORDS of WAR

BY HEATHER PRINGLE

Adapted from "Lords of Creation, Lords of War," by Heather Pringle,
in National Geographic's *Mysteries of the Maya*, 2008

A KING'S MONUMENT
The Maya built the
Temple of the Great
Jaguar as a funerary
monument in the city
of Tikal to honor the
warrior king Jasaw
Chan Kawiil.

TIKAL was one of the great centers of Maya civilization. Located in what is today the northern part of Guatemala, it was a place of amazing wealth and sophistication, but Tikal's glory was not destined to last.

KINGS AND COMMONERS

In the sixth century, the Maya world was dazzling, sophisticated, and complex. All over the lowlands, from north to south, dozens of small kingdoms flowered, each ruled by a holy lord. In wealthier lands, these kings lived in fine palaces in the city centers. During the day, they sat beneath awnings in their courtyards and accepted tribute: stacks of elegant cottons and finely embroidered cloth, blocks of jade, skins of jaguars, bags of cacao beans. At night in their private rooms, they sipped bitter frothy brews of chocolate and chili. And they struck alliances with neighboring lords.

The Maya kings became patrons of the arts. Eager to outshine their rivals, they sought out the services of the finest artists of their day. They hired sculptors to decorate temples and palace walls with carvings of themselves, their ancestors, and their gods.

The growing cities buzzed with artistic life. In small workshops, artists painted scenes of kings and nobles and palace life on vases and cups. Artists bound the feathers of tropical birds into elaborate headdresses or capes for the king and his family. Jewelers spent hours grinding blocks of jade into finery and turning out small statues, masks, even dental **inlays**. When a king smiled, his subjects sometimes glimpsed jade.

The inner hub of a Maya city was made up of palaces, pyramids, workshops, and plazas. Beyond lay the residential districts where commoners lived in small stone or adobe houses set among gardens and fields. They fertilized the soil with **compost** and animal waste and rotated their crops. As the cities grew, farmers found new ways of bringing **marginal** lands into production. They dug irrigation canals to water drier soils and built terraces on steep hillsides. In some marshy areas, they dug drainage ditches and piled up earth to make raised fields.

Most families made things to trade at local markets—knives, tools for grinding corn, woven cloth. In good years farmers sold surplus corn to merchants for items such as jade beads or cacao beans. These items held their value and were always in demand. In years when the local harvest failed, they could trade the jade and cacao for corn imported from other kingdoms.

Kings and commoners lived in separate worlds. But the two regularly came together to celebrate ancient rituals. As musicians played, the king appeared in ceremonial robes of brilliant green feathers and performed the story of the maize god. Afterward, king, queen, nobles, and commoners alike gathered on the plaza. They feasted on tamales and other foods supplied by the palace kitchens.

During this period, the city of Tikal stood out for its wealth and grandeur. In A.D. 537, a new king named Wak Chan Kawiil took the throne of Tikal upon the death of his sister. At court, some nobles watched him warily. They suspected that the 33-year-old Lady of Tikal had not died of natural causes and that their new king might have been involved in some way with her death. Wak Chan Kawiil, however, likely ignored their suspicions. He was, after all, the son of a Tikal king and an ally of a powerful royal house in Mexico. Wak Chan Kawiil seems to have longed for power and glory. Instead, his reign opened one of the darkest chapters in Tikal's history.

RIVAL KINGDOMS

When Wak Chan Kawiil took the throne, Tikal was the richest and most powerful of all the Maya kingdoms, encompassing large marshlands with fertile soils. Also, the city was located on a major divide separating the rivers that flowed to the Caribbean and those that flowed to the Gulf Coast. River traders carrying goods from one side of the divide to the other often had to transport their cargo across land for part of the way. The kingdom of Tikal controlled their **portage** routes. Furthermore, Tikal's royal house had made trade connections with the greatest commercial power in the Mexican highlands, the city of Teotihuacán (tay-oh-tee-wah-KAHN).

Wak Chan Kawiil's kingdom flourished. But signs of serious trouble were beginning to emerge in the Maya realm. The Maya were growing far too numerous, straining the land and water. In the comfort of their palaces, powerful rulers were becoming more warlike. They began eyeing the fertile fields of neighboring kingdoms.

To the north of Tikal was the kingdom of Calakmul, a combative superpower and Tikal's greatest rival. Like Tikal, Calakmul had great natural wealth. Its capital too bristled with pyramids and palaces. But Calakmul's rulers were ambitious men and women who schemed to extend their territory and exact tribute from their neighbors. The great lord of Tikal and his allies stood squarely in their way.

Calakmul's rulers set about making deals with kingdoms friendly to Wak Chan Kawiil. One by one, Tikal's allies changed sides. This strategy isolated Tikal, making it vulnerable to attack. Finally, in 562, Calakmul decided to strike. Its king picked a date on the Maya calendar when Venus, the planet of war, appeared to stand still in the night sky. This date was considered a favorable time for war.

No detailed descriptions of the battle have survived. But murals of the period have allowed archaeologists to reconstruct key details of Maya warfare. The king of Calakmul probably sent an army of warriors numbering in the thousands.

CALAKMUL TODAY
The archaeological site of Calakmul, in Mexico, is part of a large ecological reserve, protected for archaeologists to study and visitors to enjoy.

The senior officers dressed for battle in elaborate headdresses and animal pelts. They led well-armed soldiers who fought as individuals rather than as disciplined units. Using short, stabbing spears and axes, the attackers overran Tikal's defenses. They seem to have captured Wak Chan Kawiil himself, likely offering him as a sacrifice soon after. Maya scribes recorded this event with a symbol reserved for total defeat. It showed a star splashing Earth with blood or water.

After Tikal's defeat, Calakmul was the most important kingdom of the Maya world. But victory did not introduce an era of peace. Over the next century and a half, Calakmul's restless kings continued to seek ever-greater power. When **intrigue** failed, war followed. The growing strife interfered with vital trade that normally kept Maya farmers alive in times of drought and famine. Moreover, the royal house of Calakmul had made a fateful error in humiliating its old enemy. Tikal's new kings could not forget the great insult. Maya society, explains archaeologist Stephen Houston, was "highly concerned with personal honor and vengeance."

On August 5, 695, Tikal's ruler, Jasaw Chan Kawiil, struck back. Mounting a massive attack on the lord of Calakmul, Jasaw Chan Kawiil gained a great victory. A month later he celebrated his triumph in Tikal. He rode on a giant battle platform he had captured from the enemy and sacrificed his captives to the gods.

TROUBLE IN THE LAND

No amount of bloodshed could solve the increasing troubles in the lowlands. By the end of the eighth century, excess ruled the land. Maya kings demanded crushing labor from their subjects in order to construct high, defensive walls and grand pyramids. Families were chopping down too much of the forest for heat and cooking, and farmers were trying to squeeze too much food from the land. In Tikal alone, as many as 92,000 people jostled for space. Throughout the Maya lowlands, an increasingly large population crowded onto farmlands. In many areas only small stands of trees remained around Maya cities.

However, worse was to come. Around 810 a terrible drought struck. It lasted roughly nine years. Other droughts followed. In 860 the rains stopped for three years. In 910 they ceased for another six. Those who remained at Tikal and Calakmul watched in despair as famine stalked the land. Vast numbers of people died. Others set off as refugees in search of greener lands. When the rains finally returned, a few survivors crept back to Tikal. They moved into the old royal palaces and occupied rooms from which mighty kings once ruled. But they could not restore the glory of the holy lords. That had vanished forever.

THINK ABOUT IT! ||||||||||||||||||||||||||||||

1 Summarize Describe in your own words the reign of Wak Chan Kawiil and his impact on the kingdom of Tikal.

2 Analyze Cause and Effect What are some reasons why the Maya became so prosperous?

3 Evaluate Each of the following contributed to the downfall of Tikal: the actions of the kings and leaders, enemies from outside Tikal, forces beyond human control. Which do you think was most responsible?

BACKGROUND & VOCABULARY

compost *n.* (KAHM-pohst) a mixture of organic decaying matter such as leaves or grass clippings, used to fertilize or improve soil

inlay *n.* (IHN-lay) a substance shaped to fit cavities or holes and cemented into place

intrigue *n.* (IHN-treeg) a plot; secret and involved scheme

marginal *adj.* (MAR-jihn-uhl) barely acceptable; close to the lower limit of acceptability

portage *n.* (POR-tihj) a place where goods can be carried overland from one body of water to another

A Gift from the Gods: Chocolate

BY A. R. WILLIAMS

Adapted from "A Gift from the Gods: Chocolate," by A. R. Williams, in National Geographic's *Mysteries of the Maya*, 2008

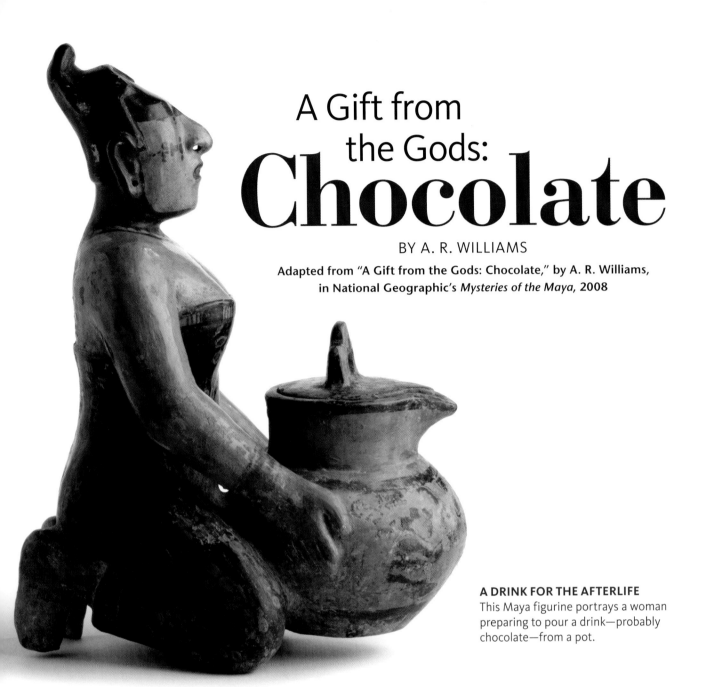

A DRINK FOR THE AFTERLIFE
This Maya figurine portrays a woman preparing to pour a drink—probably chocolate—from a pot.

FOR THE MAYA, money grew on trees—cacao trees, that is, the source of chocolate. Inside the football-shaped pods that sprout from cacao trunks and branches lie rows of seeds. Those seeds, often called beans, were among the most desired products that the Maya traded in their own region and beyond. The seeds also served as money throughout the realm. From the Maya, cacao—and chocolate—spread throughout the western world.

Native to the tropics of the Americas, cacao trees thrive in rain forests beneath the shade of taller plants. Nobody knows who first grew cacao.

The word itself traces back to the Maya word *kakaw.* By about 1100 B.C. the early Maya were making a cacao brew. In time, they produced the first hot chocolate. The thick, bitter drink was used especially for rites of passage—birth, marriage, joining the priesthood, even entry into the afterlife. The Maya recipe began with drying, roasting, and grinding fermented cacao seeds. Then they mixed the resulting powder with water and flavorings: cinnamon, chilies, and vanilla. They poured the mixture back and forth between pots, creating a cap of foam that was considered the most delicious part.

CHOCOLATE ART
Chocolate was a frequent theme in Maya art. The scene to the left is from a Maya vase and depicts a woman pouring a chocolate beverage. Above, a vessel takes the form of a goddess from whom pods sprout, much as they do from a cacao tree's branches and trunk.

Many vessels created for storing and serving spiced chocolate show scenes of kings and nobles drinking it, as well as the gods. Commoners may also have drunk chocolate during feast days. Some vessels were personalized with symbols that read, "This is my chocolate pot."

The Maya continued to export cacao even after many of their cities had collapsed. The Aztec of central Mexico became important clients. They valued the substance as the Maya did but couldn't grow it in their cool, dry climate. The Aztec depended on the Maya to provide them with cacao.

By the late 16th century, the Spanish were shipping cacao seeds back to Europe. In 1847 Englishman Joseph Fry invented the solid chocolate candy that is enjoyed around the world today. Cacao still provides income to modern-day Maya who cultivate the sacred crop.

THINK ABOUT IT! |||||||||||||||||||||||||||||||

Synthesize What made cacao a "sacred crop" for the Maya? Support your answer with details from the article.

Trade and Intrigue in the North

BY HEATHER PRINGLE

Adapted from "Trade and Intrigue: The Merchant Princes,"
by Heather Pringle, in National Geographic's *Mysteries of the Maya*, 2008

YUCATÁN POWER
The Temple of the Warriors
at Chichén Itzá displayed the
Yucatán Maya's military strength.
Archaeologists still do not fully
understand why this once-powerful
city collapsed around 1200.

WHILE DROUGHT brought much of the Maya world to its knees, the northern edges of the Maya territories remained green and prosperous. The mighty city of Chichén Itzá dominated this land of wealth and bustling trade.

THE GREATEST NORTHERN CITY

Parched and weary, some survivors of the great droughts in the Maya heartland made their way north. Perhaps stories of prosperous new cities drew them to a **peninsula** which, in the tenth century A.D., was the northern fringe of the Maya world. Some must have wondered whether they were chasing a dream. But when they arrived to the Yucatán Peninsula, they saw wondrous sights: green fields, well-stocked markets, and thriving cities. Modest rains still fell there, and the clever Yucatán Maya stored water in underground tanks hollowed out of stone.

The Yucatán Maya were also skilled traders. Merchants traveled the coast and rivers in large canoes, carrying salt, shells, cotton clothing, and bags of cacao. The refugees from the south had left behind crumbling cities and starving populations. Here, on the other side of the dusty scrub forests, was a civilization at its height.

The name of the great city of Chichén Itzá (CHEE-chuhn EET-zah) was on the lips of everyone the refugees met. Founded in the late eighth century, Chichén Itzá had flowered spectacularly in just one century. It attracted travelers, traders, and **pilgrims** from all over the peninsula. The city was wealthy and cultured. Its elegant public buildings—pyramids and temples, residences and astronomical observatories— delighted the eye. It boasted two large natural wells, each one big enough to supply all the city's inhabitants with the water they needed.

The people of Chichén Itzá worshipped a god they called Kukulkán. In the Mexican highlands, the same god was known as Quetzalcoatl (keht-zahl-koh-AH-tuhl), or the Feathered Serpent.

Dangerous and beautiful, the Feathered Serpent was both a god of war and a god of creation. He inspired warriors, yet he also watered the cornfields and protected long-distance traders. To gain power and respect, kings, merchants, and warriors linked themselves to this ancient god. Chichén Itzá was a major center for the worship of Kukulkán.

The worship of the Feathered Serpent spread rapidly throughout the Yucatán Peninsula. Followers of the new religion from Uxmal and other Maya cities made **pilgrimages** to Chichén Itzá. They threw human sacrifices and precious offerings into the waters of the sacred wells. The offerings included jade statues and wooden, copper, and gold ornaments. Many bore images of warriors and, of course, the Feathered Serpent.

RISE AND FALL

Chichén Itzá was a religious center. But it was also a city of warriors where artists celebrated both the fury and triumph of war. Inside the Upper Temple of the Jaguars, for example, artists portrayed armies destroying villages and laying siege to cities. Giant feathered serpents were shown aiding and protecting the armies. In the center of the city, sculptors carved an extensive wall with images of human skulls on spears. By such bloody means, Chichén Itzá forged the largest Maya state of all.

Chichén Itzá's network of allies helped the city expand as a commercial power. Merchants built ports for oceangoing canoes. They invested in warehouses and storage facilities. On an island

STONE GUARDIAN
A figure called a *chacmool* guards the Temple of the Warriors at Chichén Itzá. Archaeologists believe the Maya left gifts to their gods in the cups chacmools hold on their bellies.

off the northern coast, they constructed docks and piers. Traders across the region dealt in a variety of wares. But their chief local product was a mineral that one archaeologist called the "white gold of the ancient Maya." This was salt, which fishermen used to preserve their catch for shipment inland.

Chichén Itzá's merchants controlled a massive salt production facility at the coastal port of Emal. There, laborers enclosed pools of saltwater behind stone **dikes**. The sun evaporated the water, and salt caked at the bottom. Emal's salt pans covered more than 60 acres. They produced an estimated 5,500 tons of salt each year.

All this prosperity could not save Chichén Itzá from its quarreling nobility. Stories that the Maya later told speak of political intrigue, even

the kidnapping of Chichén Itzá's queen. Maya scholar Robert Sharer believes that exiles from Chichén Itzá or a group of people unhappy with conditions there left the city for Mayapán, 60 miles to the west. The new ruler of that city then launched an attack on Chichén Itzá. Archaeologists working in Chichén Itzá have unearthed toppled statues and other signs of destruction. But they don't know whether this looting took place during a war or after the city was abandoned.

What is clear is that the great city of the Feathered Serpent had collapsed by A.D. 1200. The memory of its shrines and sacred places, though, lived on among the Maya. For centuries, pilgrims continued to visit its ruins.

PLAY BALL!
Ball courts like this one at Uxmal are found in many Maya cities, including Chichén Itzá. Teams competed to hit a rubber ball through a stone ring without using their hands.

CIVILIZATION AND TRADE

For much of the 20th century, archaeologists viewed the cities that rose after Chichén Itzá as crude imitations of earlier capitals. They pointed to the thick coats of plaster that later Maya builders smoothed onto the rough walls of public buildings. Such artisans, they suggested, no longer knew how to quarry straight blocks of stone. Instead, they settled for creating the appearance of expert craftsmanship. Others saw signs of decline in the fine arts. They pointed to a sharp drop in the numbers of carved inscriptions and graceful sculptures. Early researchers had the impression that something seemed to be destroying the culture from within.

Today, archaeologists are focusing more on these later cities on the Yucatán Peninsula. As they do, they are gaining a new appreciation for their sophistication. Studies at Mayapán, for example, reveal a complex and highly structured city. Founded as early as A.D. 1050, Mayapán rose to become the greatest power in the peninsula, taking up where Chichén Itzá had left off. Mayapán's rulers laid out temples for the Feathered Serpent and a massive marketplace, palaces, plazas, roads, and archways. They built a major defensive wall around 1.6 square miles of the inner city. "It was not at all randomly put together," says American archaeologist Marilyn Masson. "There's a lot of evidence of planning."

Mayapán ruled over a group of **provinces**. Its merchant princes profited handsomely from the expanding coastal trade in salt and honey, pottery and mineral pigments, cacao and copper bells. The city likely used its warriors to support this trade. Mayapán's economy generated prosperity for its princes and also for a growing middle class. As a result, the people were no longer willing to spend long months hauling and shaping blocks of stone for vast pyramids or temples. So Mayapán's princes did away with many of the old trappings of royal power. They focused instead on creating new wealth and giving their people access to more goods. "It was fundamentally a leadership based on practical concerns," says Maya expert George Stuart.

Warring groups within the city eventually destroyed Mayapán in the middle of the 15th century. Each of the former provinces declared independence and fought to control trade. Fleeing from the fighting, many of Mayapán's residents returned to the old heartland where they founded several new kingdoms. Throughout the Maya world, warfare deepened divisions between local rulers.

Spanish armies first reached the Yucatán Peninsula in 1517. By that time, the region was already dark with betrayal and bloodshed. "But we don't know what would have happened if the Spanish had not arrived," says Robert Sharer. "At certain points every civilization has its decline. But it reaches back and grows again."

THINK ABOUT IT! |||||||||||||||||||||||||||||||||

1 Compare and Contrast This article describes the rise and fall of two great Maya cities. What did these cities have in common? In what ways were they different?

2 Synthesize The author of this article skips around in time. Describe the structure of the article in two or three sentences.

3 Make Generalizations Reread the final quotation in this article. Explain how it fits the history of the Maya covered on these pages.

MONUMENTS OF THE MAYA

Adapted from "Monuments of the Maya," in National Geographic's *Mysteries of the Maya*, 2008

The sweep of Maya history covers more than 3,500 years. It ended in the early 1500s, when Spanish conquerors put an end to a civilization in decline. Great city-states rose and fell during this long history. Archaeologists divide Maya history into three great major periods: Preclassic (2000 B.C.–A.D. 250), Classic (A.D. 250–900), and Postclassic (A.D. 900–1520). At the height of each, skilled architects and craftsmen raised pyramids to honor kings and gain favor with the gods.

EL TIGRE

The Preclassic city of El Mirador arose around 600 B.C. in a dense rain forest dotted with seasonal swamps. One of the largest buildings in the city, standing 180 feet tall, was the pyramid of El Tigre. The design of El Tigre is typical of Preclassic architecture, with two small temples and one large one. All three are set atop stepped platforms. Decorative plaster masks on the large temple had both human and cat-like elements, possibly to show the blend of religious and political power wielded by El Mirador's kings. Around A.D. 150 that political power ended. The Maya abandoned the city and most of the surrounding area.

TEMPLE OF THE GREAT JAGUAR

As El Mirador declined, Tikal thrived from around 800 B.C. to A.D. 900. The Temple of the Great Jaguar, now in ruins, still stands as a monument to the city's wealth and power. It was built to commemorate Jasaw Chan Kawiil, the 26th ruler of Tikal. Here his descendants likely held ceremonies in his honor. The building was crowned with tall roof combs carved in stone and plastered and painted. The portraits on temple combs usually showed the ruler with whom the building was associated. The pyramid's steps had inset corners with stonework that created patterns of light and shadows.

EL CASTILLO

The Postclassic city of Tulum saw its height between A.D. 1200 and 1520. It was one of the last great cities built by the Maya. Perched atop cliffs along the coast, Tulum was surrounded on three sides by a wall. The impressive central pyramid is referred to as "El Castillo." On the top platform, two rounded columns have images of feathered serpents, in honor of Kukulkán. Above the columns, three niches held statues made of stucco. The center statue is possibly the bee god. The entire pyramid may have been painted a color that is known as Maya blue. This prized color was made from the indigo plant and a clay mined on the Yucatán Peninsula.

Document-Based Question

In the early 1500s, Spanish conquistadors, or conquerors, began to arrive in Maya lands, hoping to find gold and silver there. By that time, the power of the Maya was in decline. Their great cities lay in ruins, and most of the Maya people were living in small villages and towns. Even so, it took the Spanish many expeditions and more than 170 years to conquer them. The Spanish never did find the riches they were seeking.

DOCUMENT 1 Primary Source

Bringing Disease

When the Spanish conquistadors arrived, they carried the germs of diseases such as smallpox and measles. Because the Maya had never encountered these diseases, they had no resistance to them. As a result, diseases brought over from Europe were both deadly and terrifying to the Maya. In this excerpt, a young member of the ruling family in the Maya city of Cakchiquels (KAYK-chee-kwell) recorded what happened when these diseases infected the population.

> It came from a distance. It was truly terrible when this death was sent among us by the great God. Many families bowed their heads before it. The people were seized with a chill and then a fever; blood issued from the nose; there was a cough, and the throat and nose were swollen, both in the lesser and the greater pestilence [outbreak of disease]. All here were soon attacked.

from *The Annals of the Cakchiquels by a Member of the Xahila Family*, translated by Daniel G. Brinton, 1885

CONSTRUCTED RESPONSE

1. How were the Maya affected when the Spanish spread diseases among them?

DOCUMENT 2 Primary Source

Spanish Arrival

The Chilam Balam are sacred texts of the Maya. Each Maya town collected its own text and recorded details about its religious and cultural practices and historical events. This excerpt is from the town of Chumayel. The lines tell of the experience of the people after the Spanish arrived there in 1546.

> Then . . . came the the beginning of our misery.
>
> It was the beginning of tribute [taxes] . . . the beginning of church dues . . . the beginning of strife [conflict] with blowguns . . . the beginning of robbery with violence . . . the beginning of forced debts . . . the beginning of individual strife . . .
>
> This was the origin of service to the Spaniards.

from *The Book of Chilam Balam of Chumayel*, translated by Ralph Roys, 1933

CONSTRUCTED RESPONSE

2. According to the Chilam Bilam, what did the people of Chumayel experience when the Spanish arrived?

DOCUMENT 3 Secondary Source
Battle Scene

The conquest of the Maya took many years in part because of the fierceness with which Maya fought against the Spanish. This illustration depicts the arrival of Spanish conquistador Juan de Grijalva to the Yucatán Peninsula in 1518 and the battle with Maya warriors that followed.

CONSTRUCTED RESPONSE

3. What contrasts between the Spanish conquistadors and the Maya warriors does the illlustration convey?

Spaniards Under Juan de Grijalva Land at Yucatán and Engage Maya Warriors at the Battle of Champoton, 1518

PUT IT TOGETHER

Review Think about your responses to the three questions and consider what you've learned about the Maya. Make a two-column chart with the following heads: Causes, Effects.

Cause and Effect Take notes on the problems the Spanish conquerors introduced into Maya culture and their impact. Draw on information from these documents and from articles in this book. Use your chart to organize your ideas.

Write How did the Spanish help bring an end to the Maya civilization? Write a paragraph based on the information in your chart to explain what happened. Include details from these documents and from the articles in this book.

INDEX

Alecio, Mónica Pellecer, 22
aqueduct[s], 9, 13
archaeologists, 18–23, 26, 27, 33, 35, 36
archaeology, 4, 9, 13
architecture, 36–37
art, 4, 5
  decline in, 35
astronomer[s], 13
astronomical, 17
astronomical observatory, 16, 17

ball court, 35
ball player, 4
Belize, 6–7, 16

cacao, 25, 28–29, 35
Calakmul, 26, 27
causeway[s], 17
Chac, rain god, 22
chacmool, 33
Chichén Itzá, 7, 30–35
  commercial power of, 32–33
  gods of, 31–32
  rise and fall of, 32–33
  size and importance of, 31
chocolate, 28–29
cinnabar, 6, 13
cities, 31, 35
  economy of, 35
city-state[s], 4, 20, 22
Cival, 7, 15, 16
Classic period, 6, 36, 37
climate, 15
compost, 25, 27
Copán, 7, 14
corn. See maize

Danta complex, 17
del Río, Antonio, 9
derive, 19, 22
dike[s], 33, 35
drought, 27, 31

ecological crisis, 17
El Castillo, 37
El Mirador, 7, 16, 17, 36, 37
El Salvador, 6–7
Emal, 33
enigmatic, 13
equinox[es], 15, 16, 17
excavation[s], 9, 13, 20

farming, 4, 15, 25
Feathered Serpent (Quetzalcoatl), 31, 32, 35
feathered serpents, 37
Freidel, David, 9

glyph, 12, 13
Graham, Ian, 23

Guatemala, 6–7, 8, 15, 18
  climate of, 15

Honduras, 6–7
Houston, Stephen, 27

indigo, 37
inlay, 25, 27
intrigue, 27
irrigation, 25

jade, 5, 22, 25
Jasaw Chan Kawiil, 24–27, 37

Kukulkán, 31, 32, 37

Lamanai, 16

maize, 15, 17
maize god, 16, 17, 20, 21
marginal, 25, 27
Maudslay, Alfred, 13
Maya
  arts, 4, 5, 35
  calendar, 26
  chocolate and, 28–29
  culture and society, 4, 6, 9, 13
  early theories about, 9
  farming, 15, 25
  kings/leaders/lords, 15, 17, 22, 25, 27
  mystery of, 6, 13
  painting, 20–23
  periods of history of, 6, 36–37
  writing/glyphs, 4, 12, 13
Maya blue, 37
Mayapán, 7, 33, 35
Mexico, 6–7, 13, 16
minerals, 35
mortar, 20, 22
mural[s], 18–23, 26

observatory, 16, 17

Pakal, 5, 6
Palenque, 5, 6, 7, 9–13
  first modern discovery of, 9
  study of, 13
  temple of, 10–11
peninsula, 31, 35
pilgrimage, 32, 35
pilgrim[s], 31, 35
plaster, 17, 35
population, 27
portage, 26, 27
Postclassic period, 6, 36, 37
pottery, 22
Preclassic period, 6, 16, 36
province[s], 35

pyramids, 8, 22, 27, 36–37
  Chichén Itzá, 30–35
  Cival, 15–16
  El Castillo, 37
  El Tigre, 36
  San Bartolo, 16, 20
  Temple of the Great Jaguar, 24, 37

quarry, 15, 17
Quetzalcoatl (Feathered Serpent), 31, 32

roads. See causeway[s]

sacrifice, human, 27, 32
salt, 33
San Bartolo, 7, 15, 16, 17, 18–23
  murals, 18–23
Saturno, William, National Geographic Explorer, 18–23
  interview with, 23
Sharer, Robert, 15, 33, 35
Shaw, Justine, 17
Spanish, in Mexico, 4, 9, 35, 38–39
cacao trade, 29
Stuart, George, 35

technology, new
  studying Maya history and, 13
Temple of the Great Jaguar, 24, 37
Temple of the Warriors, 30, 33
Tikal, 7, 24–27, 37
  Calakmul war with, 26–27
  location of, 26
tomb[s], 22
Tulum, 7, 37

upend[ed], 20, 22
Upper Temple of the Jaguars, 32
Uxmal, 7, 32, 34

Wak Chan Kawiil, 24–27

Yucatán Peninsula, 6–7, 31, 32, 35, 39

||||||||||||||||||||||||||||||||||||||||||||||||||||||

SKILLS

Analyze Cause and Effect, 13, 17, 27
Compare and Contrast, 35
Document-Based Question, 38–39
Draw Conclusions, 22
Evaluate, 27
Find Main Ideas and Details, 17
Form and Support Opinions, 13
Make Generalizations, 22, 35
Pose and Answer Questions, 22
Review, 39
Summarize, 17, 27
Synthesize, 29, 35
Write, 39